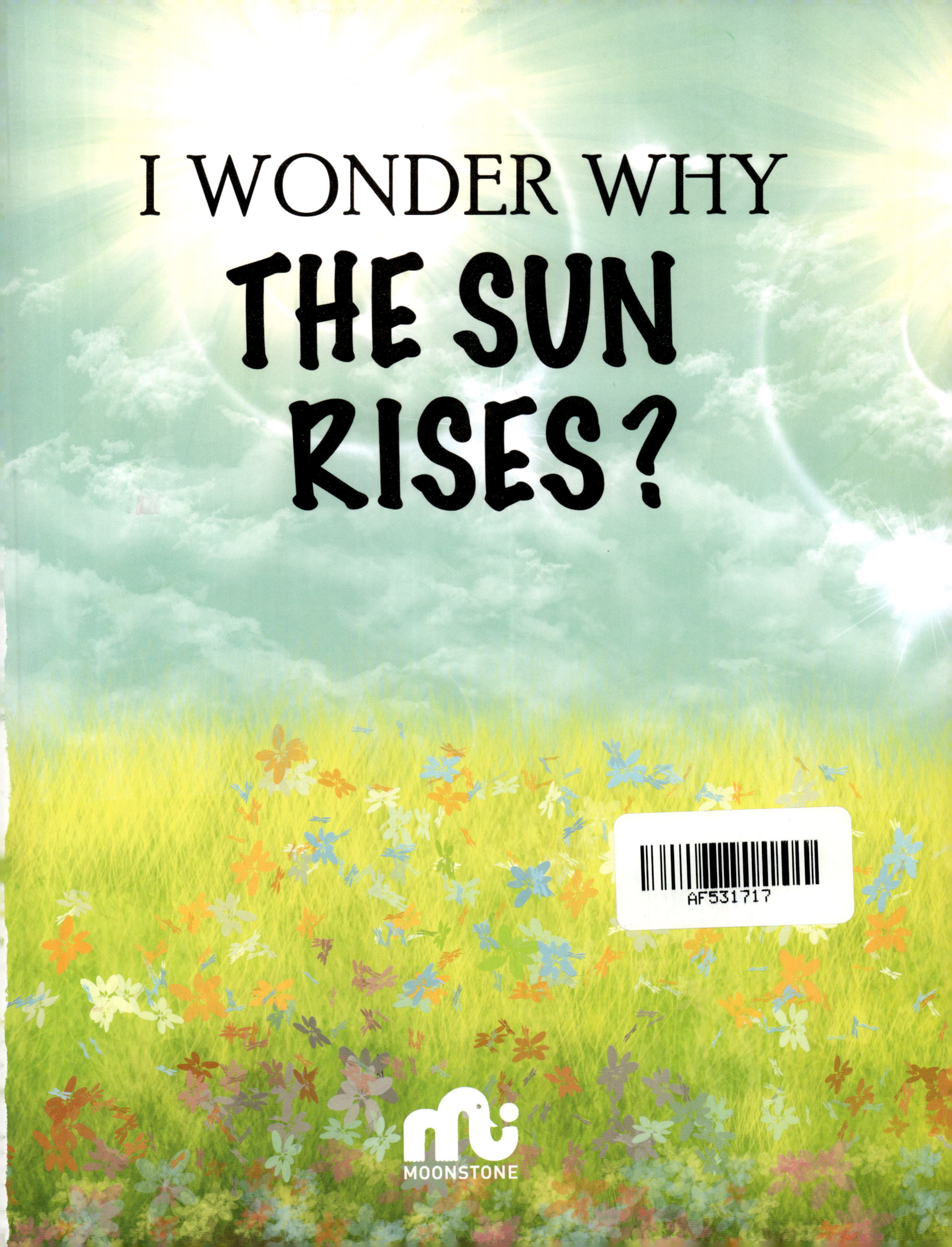
I WONDER WHY
THE SUN
RISES?
AF531717
MOONSTONE

PUBLISHED IN MOONSTONE
BY RUPA PUBLICATIONS INDIA PVT. LTD 2026
161-B/4, GULMOHAR HOUSE,
YUSUF SARAI COMMUNITY CENTRE,
NEW DELHI 110049

SALES CENTRES:
BENGALURU CHENNAI
HYDERABAD KOLKATA MUMBAI

P-ISBN: 978-93-7003-326-9
E-ISBN: 978-93-7003-699-4
FIRST IMPRESSION 2026

10 9 8 7 6 5 4 3 2 1

PRINTED IN INDIA

Table Of Contents

Why Does the Sun Rise ?

Did the sun move up into the sky ?

NOT REALLY! THE SUN ISN'T CLIMBING AT ALL–IT'S EARTH SPINNING ON ITS AXIS. AS OUR PLANET TURNS, DIFFERENT PLACES ROLL INTO SUNLIGHT, MAKING THE SUN APPEAR TO RISE.

Why does it always rise in the east ?

BECAUSE EARTH SPINS FROM WEST TO EAST. WHEREVER YOU ARE, THE FIRST LIGHT OF DAY WILL APPEAR INTHE EAST AND VANISH IN THE WEST, MARKING THE SUN'S STEADY PATH.

Does the sun move at all ?

YES, THOUGH VERY SLOWLY. THE SUN ITSELF ORBITS THE CENTRE OF OUR GALAXY, THE MILKY WAY. THIS JOURNEY TAKES HUNDREDS OF MILLIONS OF YEARS, FAR LONGER THAN A LIFETIME.

Would the sun rise if Earth didn't spin ?

NO. ONE SIDE OF EARTH WOULD ALWAYS FACE THE SUN, BAKED IN CONSTANT DAYLIGHT, WHILE THE OTHER REMAINED FROZEN IN ENDLESS NIGHT. LIFE COULDN'T SURVIVE SUCH EXTREME CONDITIONS.

What Makes Day and Night?

Why does it get dark at night?

AS EARTH TURNS, YOUR PART OF THE WORLD SLOWLY FACES AWAY FROM THE SUN. THE LIGHT FADES, SHADOWS LENGTHEN, AND EVENTUALLY THE SKY DARKENS INTO THE QUIET OF NIGHT.

Is night the same length everywhere?

NO. AT THE EQUATOR, DAYS AND NIGHTS ARE ABOUT EQUAL ALL YEAR. NEAR THE POLES, THOUGH, SUMMERCAN BRING MONTHS OF DAYLIGHT WHILE WINTER BRINGS MONTHS OF DARKNESS.

Can we see the sun at night from space ?

ASTRONAUTS CIRCLING EARTH SEE MANY SUNRISES AND SUNSETS EVERY DAY. FROM THEIR VIEW, EARTH SPINS SO QUICKLY THAT THE SUN DIPS AND RETURNS AGAIN WITHIN JUST HOURS.

What if the sun never set ?

WITHOUT NIGHT, PLANTS, ANIMALS, AND PEOPLE WOULD STRUGGLE. WE NEED DARKNESS TO REST, SLEEP, AND RECOVER. WITHOUT THAT RHYTHM, BODIES AND ECOSYSTEMS WOULD LOSE THEIR BALANCE AND ENERGY.

How Fast Does Earth Spin?

How long does one spin take ?

EARTH COMPLETES ONE FULL ROTATION EVERY 24 HOURS. THAT SINGLE SPIN GIVES US BOTH DAY ANDNIGHT, DIVIDING TIME INTO THE FAMILIAR RHYTHM OF MORNINGS, AFTERNOONS, EVENINGS, AND NIGHTS.

AT THE EQUATOR, EARTH SPINS AT ABOUT 1,670 KILOMETRES PER HOUR. THAT'S FASTER THAN A JET PLANE, BUT WE DON'T NOTICE BECAUSE EVERYTHING AROUND US MOVES TOGETHER.

Why don't we feel the spin ?

BECAUSE THE ATMOSPHERE, OCEANS, AND LAND ALL ROTATE AT THE SAME SPEED. WE ARE CARRIED SMOOTHLY ALONG WITH THEM, SO THE MOTION FEELS STEADY AND GOES UNNOTICED.

Would we fly off if Earth spun faster ?

NO, GRAVITY HOLDS US FIRMLY TO THE GROUND. EVEN IF EARTH SPUN MORE QUICKLY, ITS PULL IS STRONG ENOUGH TO KEEP US, THE OCEANS, AND THE AIR IN PLACE.

Why Is Sunrise Colourful ?

Why is the sky pink and orange at sunrise ?

AS SUNLIGHT TRAVELS THROUGH THE THICK ATMOSPHERE AT DAWN, BLUE LIGHT SCATTERS AWAY, LEAVING LONGER WAVELENGTHS–REDS, ORANGES, AND PINKS–THAT PAINT THE SKY WITH BRILLIANT MORNING COLOURS.

Are sunsets the same ?

YES, SUNSETS GLOW WITH SIMILAR SHADES FOR THE SAME REASON. AT BOTH SUNRISE AND SUNSET, THE SUN'S LIGHT HAS TO TRAVEL FURTHER THROUGH EARTH'S ATMOSPHERE BEFORE REACHING OUR EYES.

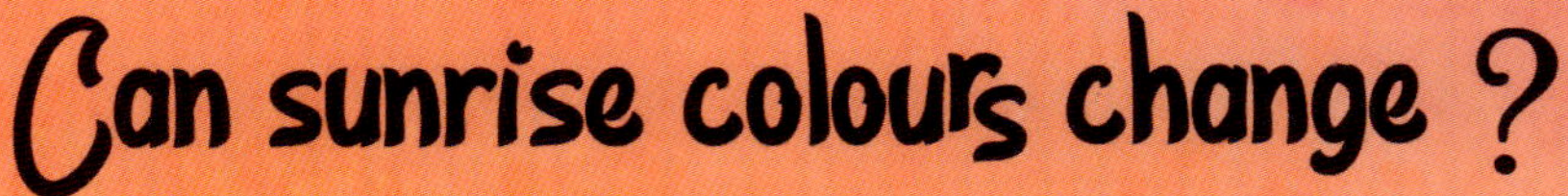

Can sunrise colours change ?

YES. DUST, SMOKE, CLOUDS, OR EVEN VOLCANIC ASH CAN SCATTER LIGHT DIFFERENTLY, CREATING SKIES OF DEEP RED, FIERY PURPLE, OR GOLDEN YELLOW, EACH MORNING LOOKING UNIQUE AND UNPREDICTABLE.

Does it always look colourful ?

NO, SOMETIMES CLOUDS COVER THE HORIZON, LEAVING THE SUNRISE GREY AND DIM. ON CLEAR MORNINGS, HOWEVER, THE COLOURS STRETCH WIDE ACROSS THE SKY, BRIGHTENING THE WHOLE WORLD.

How Important Is the Sun ?

Why do we need the sun?

THE SUN PROVIDES EARTH WITH LIGHT AND WARMTH. WITHOUT IT, SEAS WOULD FREEZE, PLANTS WOULDN'T GROW, AND ANIMALS, INCLUDING HUMANS, COULD NOT SURVIVE IN THE COLD, EMPTY DARKNESS.

Could life survive without it ?

NOT ON EARTH'S SURFACE. WITHOUT THE SUN, TEMPERATURES WOULD PLUMMET BELOW FREEZING, OCEANS WOULD SOLIDIFY INTO ICE, AND NEARLY ALL LIFE WOULD VANISH, LEAVING ONLY DARKNESS AND SILENCE.

Do plants use sunlight ?

YES. THROUGH PHOTOSYNTHESIS, PLANTS CAPTURE SUNLIGHT AND TURN IT INTO FOOD. THIS PROCESS RELEASES OXYGEN INTO THE AIR AND PROVIDES THE ENERGY THAT SUSTAINS ALMOST ALL LIVING CREATURES.

Do we eat sunlight too ?

YES, INDIRECTLY. WHEN WE EAT PLANTS OR ANIMALS THAT EAT PLANTS, WE CONSUME ENERGY ORIGINALLY STORED FROM SUNLIGHT. EVERY MEAL WE EAT TRACES BACK TO THE SUN'S STEADY POWER.

Why Is the Sun So Hot ?

What makes the sun burn ?

THE SUN IS A GIANT BALL OF GAS. INSIDE, HYDROGEN ATOMS SMASH TOGETHER TO FORM HELIUM IN APROCESS CALLED NUCLEAR FUSION, RELEASING ENORMOUS AMOUNTS OF ENERGY AS LIGHT.

How hot is it ?

THE SUN'S SURFACE REACHES ABOUT 5,500 DEGREES CELSIUS, HOT ENOUGH TO MELT METAL INSTANTLY. ITS CORE, WHERE FUSION HAPPENS, IS MILLIONS OF DEGREES—FAR HOTTER THAN ANYTHING ON EARTH.

Can we ever touch it ?

NO, THE SUN IS FAR TOO HOT AND 150 MILLION KILOMETRES AWAY. EVEN SPACECRAFT CAN ONLY GET SO CLOSE BEFORE ITS FIERCE HEAT AND RADIATION BECOME UNBEARABLE.

Why don't we burn up on Earth ?

EARTH'S GREAT DISTANCE FROM THE SUN, COMBINED WITH OUR PROTECTIVE ATMOSPHERE, SHIELDS US. THE WARMTH WE RECEIVE IS JUST ENOUGH FOR LIFE, WITHOUT SCORCHING THE PLANET COMPLETELY.

Why Does the Sun Look Different ?

Why does the sun look small ?

THE SUN LOOKS TINY BECAUSE IT'S SO FAR AWAY. IN TRUTH, IT'S ENORMOUS–OVER A MILLION EARTHS COULD FIT INSIDE IT. DISTANCE SHRINKS ITS APPEARANCE IN OUR SKY.

Why is the sun round ?

THE SUN'S GRAVITY PULLS ITS HOT GASES EQUALLY IN EVERY DIRECTION. THIS STRONG INWARD PULL GIVES IT A NEARLY PERFECT BALL SHAPE, LIKE A GLOWING SPHERE FLOATING IN SPACE.

Can we look at the sun?

NEVER DIRECTLY. ITS LIGHT IS SO BRIGHT IT CAN DAMAGE OUR EYES. SAFE VIEWING REQUIRES FILTERS, SPECIAL GLASSES, OR REFLECTED IMAGES MADE WITH PROPER EQUIPMENT.

Why does the sun look bigger at sunrise?

IT'S AN OPTICAL ILLUSION. NEAR THE HORIZON, THE SUN SEEMS LARGER BECAUSE OUR BRAINS COMPARE IT WITH TREES AND BUILDINGS. IN TRUTH, IT HASN'T CHANGED SIZE AT ALL.

Do Animals Notice Sunrise ?

Do animals wake with the sun ?

YES. MANY ANIMALS USE THE SUNRISE AS THEIR ALARM CLOCK. BIRDS BEGIN SINGING, ROOSTERS CROW, AND INSECTS STIR, ALL TRIGGERED BY THE CHANGING LIGHT OF EARLY MORNING.

What about night animals ?

NOCTURNAL ANIMALS DO THE OPPOSITE. OWLS, BATS, AND MOTHS RETURN TO REST AT SUNRISE. FOR THEM, DAYLIGHT SIGNALS BEDTIME, WHILE SUNSET MARKS THE START OF THEIR BUSY HOURS.

Do plants notice sunrise?

YES. MANY FLOWERS OPEN IN THE MORNING AND CLOSE AT NIGHT, GUIDED BY THE SUN. SUNFLOWERS EVEN TURN THEIR HEADS TO FOLLOW THE SUN'S PATH ACROSS THE SKY.

Do people's bodies follow the sun?

YES. OUR INTERNAL "BODY CLOCKS" RESPOND TO LIGHT. SUNLIGHT TELLS US WHEN TO WAKE, WHEN TO SLEEP, AND EVEN HELPS CONTROL MOODS, ENERGY, AND GROWTH THROUGHOUT OUR LIVES.

Why Does the Sun Move Across the Sky?

Is the sun really moving?

NOT IN THE WAY IT SEEMS. EARTH'S SPIN MAKES THE SUN APPEAR TO RISE, CLIMB, AND SET, THOUGH IT'S REALLY OUR PLANET TURNING BENEATH THE STEADY SUNLIGHT.

Why is it higher at noon?

AT MIDDAY, YOUR PART OF EARTH FACES THE SUN MOST DIRECTLY. THAT'S WHY THE LIGHT FEELS STRONGER, SHADOWS ARE SHORTER, AND TEMPERATURES CLIMB HIGHER COMPARED WITH MORNING OR EVENING.

Why is the sun lower in winter?

EARTH TILTS ON ITS AXIS. IN WINTER, YOUR REGION TILTS AWAY FROM THE SUN, SO IT RISES LOWER ND SHINES LESS STRONGLY, GIVING COLDER, SHORTER DAYS.

Does the sun move differently around the world?

YES. NEAR THE EQUATOR, THE SUN CLIMBS HIGH OVERHEAD, SHINING FIERCELY. NEAR THE POLES, IT STAYS LOWER IN THE SKY, GIVING LONG SHADOWS AND WEAKER WARMTH EVEN IN SUMMER.

Do All Places See the Same Sunrise?

Does the sun rise at the same time everywhere?

NO. THE WORLD IS DIVIDED INTO TIME ZONES. WHEN THE SUN RISES FOR ONE PLACE, IT MAY ALREADY BE NOON OR NIGHT IN ANOTHER PART OF THE GLOBE.

Can the sun rise at midnight?

YES, IN SUMMER NEAR THE NORTH POLE. THE SUN NEVER FULLY SETS AND INSTEAD CIRCLES THE HORIZON, GIVING THE STRANGE AND MAGICAL EXPERIENCE KNOWN AS THE "MIDNIGHT SUN."

What about polar night?

IN WINTER, THE SAME REGIONS MAY FACE AWAY FROM THE SUN FOR WEEKS. THIS "POLAR NIGHT" LEAVES COMMUNITIES IN DARKNESS, WITH ONLY MOONLIGHT AND STARLIGHT FOR COMFORT.

Why do we change clocks for daylight saving?

IN SOME COUNTRIES, CLOCKS SHIFT FORWARD OR BACK TO GIVE PEOPLE MORE DAYLIGHT IN THEIR EVENINGS. IT HELPS SAVE ENERGY AND MAKES BETTER USE OF SUNLIGHT HOURS.

What Makes Shadows at Sunrise ?

Why are shadows long in the morning ?

AT SUNRISE, THE SUN SITS LOW ON THE HORIZON. LIGHT SHINES SIDEWAYS, STRETCHING SHADOWS ACROSS THE GROUND SO THEY LOOK TALL, LONG, AND SOMETIMES VERY DRAMATIC

Do shadows move ?

YES. AS THE SUN CLIMBS HIGHER, SHADOWS SLOWLY CHANGE DIRECTION AND LENGTH. WATCHING THEM IS LIKE WATCHING THE SUN'S JOURNEY WRITTEN QUIETLY ACROSS THE GROUND BENEATH OUR FEET.

Can shadows tell time ?

YES. PEOPLE ONCE USED SUNDIALS—STONE OR METAL DISCS MARKED WITH NUMBERS. A STICK IN THE CENTRE CAST A SHADOW, MOVING HOUR BY HOUR AS THE SUN TRAVELLED ACROSS THE SKY.

Do shadows vanish?

ALMOST. AT NOON, SHADOWS ARE AT THEIR SHORTEST AND MAY LOOK AS IF THEY'VE DISAPPEARED. BUT THEY NEVER GO COMPLETELY, BECAUSE SUNLIGHT ALWAYS STRIKES AT SOME SMALL ANGLE.

What If the Sun Didn't Rise?

Could the sun stop rising one day?

NOT AS LONG AS EARTH SPINS STEADILY. EACH ROTATION GUARANTEES THE CYCLE OF SUNRISE AND SUNSET, MARKING THE DAYS AND NIGHTS THAT GIVE OUR LIVES RHYTHM AND BALANCE.

How long would light last?

ONLY EIGHT MINUTES. THAT'S HOW LONG SUNLIGHT TAKES TO TRAVEL 150 MILLION KILOMETRES FROM THE SUN TO EARTH. AFTER THAT, THE WORLD WOULD BE DARK FOREVER.

Do other planets have sunrises?

YES, EVERY PLANET SPINS, SO EACH HAS ITS OWN SUNRISE AND SUNSET. ON MARS, FOR EXAMPLE, THE RISING SUN GLOWS PALE BLUE INSTEAD OF FIERY ORANGE OR RED.

What if the sun suddenly vanished?

EARTH WOULD BE PLUNGED INTO COLD, SILENT DARKNESS. WITHIN WEEKS, OCEANS WOULD FREEZE SOLID. ALMOST ALL LIVING CREATURES WOULD DIE, UNABLE TO SURVIVE WITHOUT LIGHT AND WARMTH.

How Did People Explain Sunrise Long Ago ?

Did ancient people have ideas ?

YES. LONG BEFORE SCIENCE, PEOPLE TOLD STORIES ABOUT THE SUN'S JOURNEY. THEY EXPLAINED ITS DAILY RISE AND FALL WITH MYTHS, LEGENDS, AND POWERFUL GODS OR MAGICAL CREATURES.

What kinds of stories ?

SOME SAID A SUN GOD SAILED ACROSS THE SKY IN A FIERY BOAT. OTHERS IMAGINED A MIGHTY BIRD DRAGGING THE SUN OR A GIANT HORSE PULLING IT IN A CHARIOT.

Do we still tell them?

YES. MYTHS ABOUT THE SUN LIVE ON IN BOOKS, PLAYS, AND ART. THEY REMIND US OF HUMAN IMAGINATION AND OUR TIMELESS WONDER AT THE RISING AND SETTING SUN.

Why tell stories?

STORIES HELPED PEOPLE EXPLAIN THE MYSTERIES OF NATURE. SUN MYTHS GAVE COMFORT, GUIDANCE, AND MEANING TO DAILY LIFE BEFORE SCIENCE EXPLAINED THE TRUE REASONS FOR SUNRISE AND SUNSET.

Will the Sun Rise Forever ?

Will the sun always rise each day ?

YES, FOR BILLIONS OF YEARS TO COME. THE SUN STILL HAS PLENTY OF FUEL TO BURN, AND EARTH WILL KEEP SPINNING, GIVING US SUNRISES AND SUNSETS EVERY SINGLE DAY.

Can the sun burn out ?

ONE DAY, FAR IN THE FUTURE, THE SUN WILL RUN OUT OF FUEL. WHEN THAT HAPPENS, IT WILL SWELL INTO A RED GIANT STAR, CHANGING THE SOLAR SYSTEM FOREVER.

Should we worry?

NO. THAT TRANSFORMATION WON'T HAPPEN FOR ABOUT FIVE BILLION YEARS. HUMANITY HAS PLENTY OF TIME TO GROW, EXPLORE, AND POSSIBLY FIND NEW HOMES AMONG THE STARS.

What will happen then?

AFTER SWELLING, THE SUN WILL SHRINK INTO A WHITE DWARF, GLOWING FAINTLY. BY THEN, HUMANS MAY LIVE FAR BEYOND EARTH, CARRYING SUNLIGHT'S LESSONS INTO DISTANT GALAXIES.

A mini quiz :

Why does the sun look like it rises in the east ?

____

What makes sunrise skies so colourful ?

____

How long does sunlight take to reach Earth ?

____

What do plants do with sunlight ?

____